DARWIN SUR

For Kate

Darwin Survivor

NEIL ASTLEY

PETERLOO POETS

First published in 1988
by Peterloo Poets
2 Kelly Gardens, Calstock, Cornwall PL18 9SA

ISBN 0 905291 97 2

Printed in Great Britain by
Latimer Trend & Company Ltd, Plymouth

ACKNOWLEDGEMENTS are due to the editors of the following publications in which some of these poems first appeared: *Agenda, Argo, Encounter, The Gregory Awards Anthology 1981 & 1982* (Carcanet/Society of Authors, 1982), *Harry's Hand, The Honest Ulsterman, Iron, Literary Horizons* (India), *The Literary Review, London Magazine, New Statesman, Ostrich, Outposts, Oxford Magazine, Pacific Quarterly* (New Zealand), *P.E.N. Broadsheet, Pick, Poetry Book Society Anthology 1988/89* (Hutchinson/PBS, 1988), *Poetry Review, Smoke* and *Stand*.

'The Mission Of Port Keats' was broadcast on *Poetry Now* (BBC Radio 3) and 'Hearing Things' appeared on a Morden Tower/CND poem-poster.

Some of these poems also appeared in a pamphlet, *The Speechless Act* (Mandeville Press, 1984), and some were included in a collection for which Neil Astley received an Eric Gregory Award in 1982.

Peterloo Poets is a list published with the assistance of South West Arts.

supported by
NORTHERN
ARTS

NEIL ASTLEY

Contents

page

9   The Speechless Act
10   Hearing Things
11   Old Misery
12   Sapphics: Hindley
13   Foreigners
14   Loyalist
15   Operation Teddy Bear
16   A Martian Sees The Earth Destroyed
18   There Is A Time
19   My Friend The Preacher
20   Deceit
21   The Summer Break
22   On A Bar Of Basil Brush Soap
24   The Great Lover At The Launderette
25   The Fish
27   Listeners
28   Dreaming
29   Foghorn
30   Sestina: Rossetti's Model
32   The Spirit Of The Place
33   The Political Climate
36   A Month In The Country
38   One Way
40   The Other Side
45   The Mission Of Port Keats
48   Two Poems For My Mother
50   Goannas
51   Darwin Cyclone
53   Darwin Survivor

54   *Notes*

'*Whereof one cannot speak, thereof one must be silent.*'
—Ludwig Wittgenstein

The Speechless Act

When words fail, or will not serve
their purpose, there are things they leave
unspoken. The harder they strain
the more they confuse what they mean
to say, which cannot be precise.
Like foreigners they compromise,
choose something with a safe consonant
that won't upset; rather than grunt
will seem to be lost for a word.
Like lovers just slightly absurd,
evasive, their talk is inexact;
in private too, the speechless act.

Hearing Things

These sounds I have to live with all my life:
as when my husband's outside chopping wood
each thud is echoed by another thud
and by the next one I am waiting for.

His saw may whine but doesn't grate the way
my father's did—it's smoother, going up
and back just like my iron on his shirt
this scraping that I cannot stop myself

from hearing as the chanting of the crowd.
They tell me it's my memory playing tricks
and yet I cannot shut it out, nor can
I stop it once I've heard that sound again.

When they were shouting at the house I held
my pillow round my head but still I felt
the muffled words, the slamming of the door.
You can't expect me to forget these things.

Where are you Mother Mother? calls my son
and I am running down the garden path
and screaming Mother what is happening?
I hear the anguish in my father's voice,

the boots that clatter on the concrete step.
But cries and weeping are just words to you.
There's no way I can speak of all I've heard
except to say that this is what I hear.

Old Misery

' "The house was like a church, for father's rule
of silence was obeyed by all of us,
upheld by things through which you felt his will.
As butterflies became his specimens,

the antique chairs, chaise-longues and tables weren't
our furniture but property, and his.
His bookshelves muffled sound, the books absorbed
our talk, the tortured portraits had his eyes.

You only had to whisper, even if
he wasn't in—and then he'd soon appear,
annoyed to find you home; or just to cough
when walking past his room and he'd be there

like Mephistopheles—with furrowed brow,
the usual show of hurt and puzzlement . . . " '
'Her very words,' I said to Jack, 'and now
you listen to Old Misery's lament . . . '

We heard him talking to his friends: he thought
she had more sense, he was surprised at her.
He said she was ungrateful, though he ought
to be relieved, there'd been an 'atmosphere'.

'More like a smell,' says Jack to me, and needs
to say no more, as when his mam abused
Old Misery for giving him his cards:
' "*Ye put our lad on t'dole, and after he'd*

been bloody working half his life for ye—
a good man who's worth more than all o'youse."
If I were young there'd be no holding me.
I'd scrape this place's shite from off me shoes.'

Sapphics: Hindley

If I feigned remorse I'd be pleading guilty
Just to find my hopes were no less unreal.
What I've kept till now to myself I won't be
    Made to reveal.

Oh they let me think there was hope, I really
Thought there was last Christmas, and it was awful
When I heard, I struggled to breathe, could barely
    Speak, it was cruel.

Silence walled them out of my head and helped me
Stop them understanding me at the trial.
Saying nothing was my escape; they'd have me
    Sink to his level,

Blurting out what happened, the dogs that helped me
Clean the mess up afterwards, stuff that people
Wanted him to shock them with. But the Nazi
    Photos weren't real,

Everything was distant, it had already
Gone like childhood. Someone had dreamt this muddle,
Maybe it was him, for I dreamed he said he
    Worshipped the devil,

Would I let him enter my soul and body?
Shake the nightmare off, and be proud not feeble.
Shut your mind to it, like the dumbshow monkey
    Speaking no evil.

Foreigners

The pavement meets the house, our bedroom wall
and window, with no garden, not even
a hedge or strip of concrete inbetween.
We hear some drunkard stumbling up the hill

singing his heart out; hear him clear his throat
and half his lungs, and brace ourselves as he
attacks the highest note of *Danny Boy*—
so near he could be sitting on the bed.

You feel defenceless, naked, grip my hand
as the window shakes, as when those children
shrieking bash at the door, or when a stone
hits the pane but fails to leave it shattered.

Mud they smeared on the windows, lentils poured
through the letterbox: while we laughed at that
we found it hard to get them up with just
a brush; we picked them from our feet in bed,

shook the sheets, and wished we had a Hoover
(to hear the damned things rattle up inside
and disappear for good). And someone tried
to force the door; they've drawn a swastika

and carved NF as though those neatly linked
initials were a tribute to their love.
We heard them doing it but couldn't breathe
until they'd gone. The man upstairs goes out

to work at six, revs up his clapped-out car
and feeds us his exhaust. At nine you find
the street deserted but you know you're watched,
some curtain twitches as you shut the door;

a neighbour shuffles past with lowered eyes,
and glances back of course. Our own pretence
is not to notice theirs, oblivious
of them as of their kid's obscenities.

Loyalist

'Her majesty burned with choler that there was a book
published in print inveighing against the marriage, as
fearing the alteration of religion, which was intituled
*A gaping gulf to swallow England by a French
marriage.*'—William Camden

Giving them his hand, Stubbs murmured
a short prayer; the stench of the market
hung in the air, London blurred.

Waiting, he swayed in the heat:
then stood rigid, took the pain
in silence, eyes singing as mallet

struck knife through wrist and bone,
clean as a fowl's neck; stared,
and cried *God save the Queen!*

The left hand shook a hat,
the right lay limp in its blood.
A wild laugh stunned the crowd,
and mutely, we dispersed.

Operation Teddy Bear

they drop leaflets
to tell the dinks
they're in a movement area:
they'll have to beat feet,
get their asses out of there

they drop the ordnance
but didn't think
there'd be collateral damage:
we figured they could
read their crummy language

there's one bunch
gets out OK
they're for the relocation camp
'xcept one of the guys
who's to be neutralised:

it's this gook who
looks like a VC
and he gets interrogated,
has to be terminated
with extreme prejudice

A Martian Sees The Earth Destroyed

Cruises are trick cigars aimed at Russians,
who like that kind of joke. A batch goes off

to Moscow but the stupid blighters send
their own brand back. They make an awful bang!

After the flash there is a lot of smoke.
Women object to this: they try to stop

the men from lighting up but get arrested
by tobacco manufacturers.

Bunkers are holes where politicians go
to ground like moles, and generals have them gassed . . .

London is a *Waste Land* out of Dante's
Inferno, cleverly recalling Bosch:

perhaps the set for some disaster film,
the charring just a little overdone . . .

That bridge made one side of a rectangle.
It's now the square of the hypotenuse

and drinks the river like a shipyard crane.
Lamp-posts are Uri Geller's cutlery.

The sound effects are unbelievable:
those blasted windows must be deaf!

A vacuum cleaner bursts across the sky.
People get peppered, and then paprika'ed

with Martin Amis acne. Here a man
beheaded makes an exclamation mark!

Leather-skinned like one of Heaney's
bog people, he is a sizzling slab

of doner kebab, his pork chop fat
spits till it's burnt black and he is charcoal.

Cut! Who'll pay to see the Earth destroyed?
Flash back to Oxford, early September

during the fifth and final Test:
a patio of friends and poets down

here from the Ministry of Decadence
for the long weekend. One says such a strong

opening attack means England will collapse.
Pongo distracts them with his language games:

the dildo is an Amazon's lipstick;
a missile, making you explode inside.

Pineapples are grenades. Watch out! Marcel
the porn confectioner will better that:

the recipe for his chocolate eclairs
he learned from Freud himself. The singer smiles

as he pops Black Magic in her Mars-hole.
The verse contortionist then disappears

like Ouroboros up his own arsehole—
leaving a fart to mushroom in the air.

There Is A Time

A bitter morning, damp with mist:
they swish through the wet field
grass seeds spattered on their jeans.
The first sun glints on gunmetal churns

huddled by the gate, still waiting to be
picked up. Your man says he woke early,
his alarm the rooks' clamour breaking
with the light, but he may be lying

through his teeth. Takes his time before
he comes on her body lying where
the bracken had been broken.
The story goes she wouldn't let them

bare her legs but ordered one to press
his muzzle to her white muslin dress
making the two roses just above the hem.
She sang: To everything there is a time,

turn, turn, turn. A time for peace,
she told the cursèd vigilantes
cawing in the trees; for love and hate
a time, I swear it's not too late.

My Friend The Preacher

Tonight my friend the preacher talks to me
about the miracle of radio—
by which I'm spared the man but not his dis-
embodied drone, though able just this once
to answer back. He *speaks* the truth, he says,
yet like a foreigner his sense of stress
is out of key, as if his mind preferred
another tongue. He claims to be con*cerned*,
this pious, earnest, godless man of God,
but can't you listeners tell that he's a fraud
and putting on this saintly act? You can't
of course, but nor does he (pretending that
he's one of them) suspect the nodding friends
he thinks he knows—with whom he jokes and acts
the fool—despise him as a hypocrite;
and yet we'll tell him he was good tonight,
and sound convincing, just as *he* must if
he listens while he's speaking to himself.

Deceit

'*Try them—they have to be*
out soon.' The landlord told me
your name: '*Go now, she may*
be in . . .'
        But you weren't,
though your husband offered
to show me round; I said
I couldn't stop.
          How would you
have reacted, hearing
who'd been? . . . '*He seemed to like*
the kitchen, and the bedroom.'

Better to burn at home
beneath my other act
than be tried by your
poor innocent.
        He might
have apologised for
'our daughter's things'—bears and toys
strewn across the rush-matting,
her little clothes
hanging to dry. Then later,
perhaps, you'd have looked at her
closely, trying to keep me
out of your mind.

The Summer Break

'*Well, it's finished,*' you say, as if
it were some TV series you'd been
coming round to watch: the end so obvious
I should have seen it all along.

The man didn't convince, the passion
was hardly real—or was that just
her bad acting? I can't believe it's
the same story, the way you tell it.

Everyone's away. There's not much on:
a season of French films, the cricket
and repeats. You want to visit
castles, and Kenneth's got a car.

On A Bar Of Basil Brush Soap

1. LOVE'S DEITY
Gift of a loved one's whim, its charm
like hers is strained. How long I suffered
its face to be saved (its fate suspended,
tensed like a thread of soap film).

Expression frozen, this fox figurine
is sacrosanct, a carved idol. It grins
as always at the same joke—and glistens
with the sweat of its first violation,

looks spoiled as its clean-cut curves
leak away into a fat solution.
My final sentence is oblivion
for this relic of love: when its last drops

weep down my cheek, swell till they totter
and tear the fragile skin of the water.

2. VALEDICTION

Those ice-hard eyes and razored features
begin to soften as I work my hands
around its body, tightening my fingers
so its wee pink head pops out like a glans

and is drawn back in. Carried away,
it slides about in a mess of warm cream,
slops and slurps as if it wanted me
to keep squeezing, harder, to make it squirm.

Smeared with its own slime, slashed by my hairs,
it rests in the dish. My washes are blurring
its image, wiping that smile off its face.

I'll break it down, slowly, to nothing
but a blob: a sliver of crimson pressed
down the plug-hole, a lump in my throat.

The Great Lover At The Launderette

Slung in a rubbish bag, musty with mould,
these I have left: some odd socks stiff with dirt;
a speckled, grubby-collared cricket shirt
missing all summer, with its sleeves still rolled.

Helpless I watch them flail in their machines,
frothing at the glass, shaken, spun and drained:
a tee-shirt she hated; the sheets we stained;
limp, grey underpants; faded, patched-up jeans.

That pillow once held the scent of another
which sent me to sleep, lingering for days.
Hoping she'd come, I'd sit here in a daze
despairing *would she never let me love her?*

These are all clean now, but only at the cost
of losing her I loved and choosing her I lost.

The Fish

After the storm I found the bins filled
with water; in one of them a fish bobbed,

dead of course. Perhaps it had dropped
from the sky, I said; the others scoffed,

that kind of thing didn't happen.
Was it a sign then? I could make it mean

anything I want . . . maybe my lost soul's
in that fish, like Bidasari's—why else

should it plop into my empty bin?
Why land here and not at number ten?

And yesterday I was doodling a fish
on an envelope: add that to our list

of coincidences—one fish, as ordered.
I'd draw you, but you know I'm no good

at people; just looking at your picture
ought to make you drop by. But I'll draw

the fish while it's still recognisable,
before it shrivels up and starts to smell.

See how the fins are sleeked back; it's silvery,
with a fixed jaw. I'm tempted to say

its gaping mouth is like mine; the eyes
are round, they gawp at you. It does

look pretty awful. If you hold it
up to the light you can see inside.

There, I've finished. And now you've read this
you're looking at my drawing of the fish.

Listeners

'. . . he turned back to wave until the mist and the hill
hid him . . . Panic seized me, and I ran . . . to the top of
the hill, and stood there a moment dumbly, with
straining eyes and ears. There was nothing but the mist
and the snow and the silence of death.'—Helen Thomas

And clattering down the iron-hard lane
(avoiding the ice), he'd halt at her voice
and hear only the rush of the silence;
a tinkle of couplings, way up the line.

There the broadcast ended, before Arras
where a shell-blast would stop his heart.
The sky outside looked utter black, I thought
(you had listened and were crying, for us,

across the city): one by one the lights
flicked out, as a plane's tail ember moved
through the darkness, unswerving, and silent.

You shivered that night in your cold sheets,
your window brushed by snow. I could hear
on my pane the same breathless whisper.

Dreaming

Neither sleeping nor yet
awake, I try to hold on
to your image, now it is slipping
away. I must call out
your name, speak again
to you, as in the dream:
my mouth makes it, the soft
sound that is your word,
but you do not come.

*   *   *

In the woods my head clears.
It seems another dream, this
place of yours; again
I am a trespasser. These
massive trees that seem
somehow to hold you: how
muscular their limbs are, taut,
or sweeping.
            And I know you
in the moist nap of moss,
the rock's gaunt strength,
even in oak bark, and birches'
cracked and flaking skin.
The dark smell of the earth
is yours, the grass soaked
with dew.
            Morning sky
pale expanse cold
in the west, how
you glow above me.

Wind, take my hair,
cool my skin. Let me
feel your touch.

Foghorn

Behind our voices it moans,
unlike anything, I say,
except itself. We hear it
as we speak, calling to the sea.

The lighthouse glows,
and dies; then the foghorn
sounds through grey. We try
to take it in.

At night, I say, it reaches
into your sleep, insistent
but calming. I look at you,
we listen for it.

The light comes on: you push
my eyes away, and talk about
a search for love. I follow
your lips, absorbed.

I find your eyes, the foghorn
goes; and the windless sea
dashes itself, our light
is a flare in its spray.

The sea's not right, we'll have
to keep our distance. Why
should I mind when your voice
is pouring into me?

Sestina: Rossetti's Model

Feeling my way but not finding the poems,
I was bewildered when my efforts turned
love into sentiment; my earnest love
seemed overplayed and more like lust to her.
In love and poetry I didn't know
restraint, for everything was how it looked.

Some nights I thought the words for which I looked
rose to be felt, as if I stroked the poems
and traced them on her skin. How could I know
they'd slip away? I woke to find them turned
back into crumpled sheets, my love for her
a dream, and unbelievable as love.

I should have known I couldn't capture love;
I couldn't have the words for how she looked
at me, and what I couldn't have from her
I'd not convince her of in any poems.
So why imagine that things might have turned
out differently, despite what I now know?

Whether it could have worked I'll never know
because I lost my chance to prove my love.
Hearing me swear I'd wait for her, she turned
her head away; not caring if I looked
a fool, I said I'd show her that my poems
expressed the faith I'd always have in her.

Sometimes I think she's here, and speak to her
if I'm alone, for I want her to know
that while I've learned to write considered poems
I've not recovered from losing her love—
and how I've followed women who have looked
and moved like her, who were her as they turned

with that same sweep of flowing hair, then turned
out to be strangers. Some were so like her
that I pursued them, blindly till I looked
at how I'd painted them. Didn't I know
Dante Rossetti only had one love,
his Lizzie, whom the women in his poems

turned out to be? Christina had to know
her ghost lived in their portraits. As my love,
looked for in others, lies behind their poems.

The Spirit Of The Place

I like to drift around, to wander up
and down the country, homing in on flats
that saw me through a winter or a job
down south, to pass through rooms in those old haunts

where strangers live. My London bedsit must
frustrate another me, another youth,
unless it's been knocked down or modernised.
I don't allow for change: in Hammersmith

the men I picture working have retired;
in Sheffield pubs I hover at the bar
and look for Lynne, although she's disappeared.
When unimpaired my vision reaches far

across the Borders, up to Edinburgh
back in the summer of '76
that never ends, then down through Lancashire
to Birmingham, my father's back-to-backs.

I follow high-speed trains and motorways,
the whole of England (all but Nottingham)
below me. Bradford too is lost in haze,
the city where a girl I loved was from,

and Nottingham is where I heard she moved
(although she could in fact be anywhere).
However, if I knew for sure she lived
in Nottingham, I'd make that town appear

and see her shopping, on her way to work,
or maybe putting something in the post;
imagining I watched her, she would look
a little pale, as if I were a ghost.

The Political Climate

1.
It is a cold spring: our grey city
always wet, everyone complaining
about the food queues—

dull mornings of heartless drizzle
till the daffodils splashed yellow
across the parks.

Along the river, there are crocuses
breaking through. 'But they were planted,
it is all planned,'

you say, and then lose interest.
'I cannot sleep in this damp,
I am so tired.'

2.
The first of May: how annoyed you are,
meeting me, by chance, in the Square.

Before the tank parade they have dancing,
men in leather breeches, girls wearing

flowery cotton frocks trimmed with lace—
just like your mother's, in the old photographs.

And the songs! You feel so much better
hearing them again, as we stand together.

But you rush off. 'Please leave me alone,'
you say, quickly, 'we must not be seen.'

3.
I remember your dream. There are two men:
one wears a black trenchcoat, is sourly
watching you across a crowded room;

the other, a coarse peasant-type,
brags about the people he has shadowed—
his friends have to laugh at the story

of the poor grocer who threw himself
under a tram. And one of these it is
who comes for you each time: the footsteps

on the stairs are like mine, and the knock
is the same; you cannot tell until
you open the door, slightly, and the man

pushes his way in. The sour one is brisk:
they know I have told you about freedom,
which doesn't exist, neither do I, now.

You must go with him, for he has no choice
in the matter. There is a car outside,
you're going into internal exile.

4.

'Keep away, stop whispering.' But they know
we're friends, at least; this place is so small
that we must meet sometimes, and be seen;
avoiding each other will seem odd.

Watch now, I touch your arm, we smile
at something; we look so happy we might
even be lovers. I move closer:
'Let me help, please, I know how you feel.'

'This city is so drab . . .' is all you say—
you cannot trust anyone. The wind bites.
I do not blame you; we are all numbed.
As you walk away, the man whom we saw

with the pigeons gives you a wolf-whistle
that cuts me right to the bone.

A Month In The Country

The place is Islayev's estate in the country,
this framework his latest construction: 'That nonsense
will harness the river, and give him the freedom
to grow what he wants. If he's working he's happy.'
She turns to me, languid. His wife. And the woman
I've loved more than any. Natalya Petrovna.

'Now give me your arm,' says Natalya Petrovna,
and raises my hopes of our walk in the country.
Though close she is distant, not there, for the woman
is watching Belyaev at work on some nonsense,
a kite for Verochka to fly. She'll be happy
resisting the wind's tug, its pulling for freedom.

In falling for him she surrenders her freedom:
Belyaev is loved by Natalya Petrovna.
She too is denied, and if nobody's happy
Islayev at least is transforming the country.
But now this lament is the worst of the nonsense,
this sadness like grief, to have lost such a woman!

I only exist in my love for this woman,
in playing a part that allows me no freedom.
She tells me I'm talking a lot of old nonsense,
my speeches are lost on Natalya Petrovna.
I can't live without her. This month in the country
her presence alone makes me more than just happy.

These words are Turgenev's, who thinks he is happy
reliving his *liaison* with Pauline, the woman
he never possessed, through his *Month in the Country*.
Her husband, his friend, would allow them some freedom,
Islayev's approach with Natalya Petrovna.
'Turgenev, you write such a load of old nonsense.'

These phrases are echoes recalling a nonsense.
They signify nothing. I cannot be happy
imagining her as Natalya Petrovna.
My dreams have me never quite reaching the woman.
Each line may be mine but I don't have the freedom
to change how it ends in *A Month in the Country*.

What nonsense it is with my love for the woman:
unhappy or happy, I give up my freedom.
Natalya Petrovna. I'd give her the country.

One Way

*'I might have thrown poor words away
And been content to live'*

*

'We'll learn that sleeping isn't death'
                    —W. B. Yeats

'One way is it?' (Those words again.) *'Galway?'*
he asked again: was it one way I wanted?
'A single.' Half asleep, I heaved my case
onto the rack, and must have looked as haunted
then as the night before in Donegal
when I imagined, with the moonlit bay
glowing behind the gauze, I saw her face
out in the dark, appearing through a swirl
of cloud, then fading as the soft rain slanted
across the mountain like the spirit of the place.

Nothing touched me. The days just slipped away.
In Drumcliff churchyard I remembered Yeats's
words on death, *Ancient Ireland knew it all.*
My ticket made me think of *Galway Races,*
the disappointed patriot, his life spent
with useless words, whose love would never play
his ideal woman, though as mythical
Cathleen he'd felt the spirit of Ireland
breathe through Maud Gonne's performance, as his phrases
rose from her throat, her voice trembling for the people.

The first time guns were levelled at me
my country's soldiers were responsible.
I watched their revving armoured cars reversed
back down her roads, like one of her people
but also an intruder in their eyes,
unused to what they witnessed every day.
I wondered how she'd let herself be cast
as victim in their rescue exercise
when helicopters on the night patrol
jabbered above, and died away over Belfast.

Their murmur stalked me when I lost my way
one night in a Republican stronghold
where gunmen appeared from every gable
like wraiths, when numbed by unlit fog-filled
streets, numbed beyond shock or sense of danger,
my desolation made a ghost of me;
so drained of hope I was invisible
the other side of a one-way mirror
reflecting nothing but that frozen world
I stared into, a mourner at a funeral,

like when I'd whispered to her as she lay
asleep, as though *I love you* were a spell
to make her want the one who kissed her back
to life, whose arm her own arm wandering fell
across, who watched her coming slowly to
and saw this vigil was as much one way
as a wake, given what she'd give him back:
the hands now hovering, at a quarter to,
their last act the moment her alarm bell
rang, almost touching her face, and holding her back.

The Other Side

They stopped the barge
at Orsova, wrenched back the hatch
cursing all Slavs. I watched

one blindly point
a gun towards me, paralysed;
it caught the light, waved

like a sword
over the black hold I squatted
beast-like in. He looked right

through me
at something he could not see
or avoid; I felt him suddenly

sicken, and he had
to avert a thumping head.
We'd passed the Iron Gate, I heard

them say: no more
than two days to Bazias where
the river leaves the border

*   *   *

Days, weeks, an age
of blackness. The engine stopped
and started, senses merged

with crawling grain;
piss-rotten sacks that burst
their bellies; the current against

which we pushed
weakly, the dark rocking, aching as
I lost my mind and consciousness.

*   *   *

My white bolster
is fresh with starch, water
and cool air; there is a dresser

by the bed, polished
ebony, and the floor is beeswaxed.
I breathe in slowly because it is hard

to move without pain,
without feeling my chest pressing in.
One wall is dappled; the pattern

shifts as the curtains
stir, settle, as swaying pines
scatter the light, shadowy, resinous

* * *

Fed at first
on broth, I now eat unaided.
The woman brings black bread

with cheese or honey,
apple torte and real coffee;
and I can see her clearly,

her long hair
tied back, blonde; I've no idea
how old she is, what she does here.

She is called Karin
she tells me, talking away in German
which I don't speak yet can

understand
what she says. The house was burned
on Kristallnacht, this room was saved:

nothing else remains
but the staircase, the rest is in ruins;
it is north of Vienna, the Russians

know this is
part of their zone, but their soldiers
keep away, being superstitious.

*   *   *

Singing she rubs
a salve into my skin, her voice
is sleepy: her warm hands ease

the pain; it fades
slowly, dying away as she ends
her lieder, like my need for words.

*   *   *

The night waits.
I wake as something screeches
in the pines; so shrill is this

cry that
the trees' shadows are made
to shiver. And the walls melt

away as cloud
drifts across the moon, cutting out
its glow: a hole is created

black as jet
where the window was, is pierced
by two stabs of fierce heat,

the close-set
eyes of a screech-owl, red
as ingots. I watch it spread

its wings, am
unable to move: into the room
it swoops, onto my face to become

the woman Karin
naked and astride me, her tongue in
my mouth, when an explosion

rocks the whole
room, and we freeze. A wall
has burst, and through a pall

of smoke and dust
a man advances, black-bearded,
holding out a yellow tablet;

shrieking he
calls on angels of the Red Sea,
conjures Sinoi, Sinsinoi,

Seman-
gelaf: it is not Karin
but Karīna who cries out in

a shrill voice,
it is Lilith the succubus
who was undead who says

she only wants
to rest now, who presses
my hand. And I who act at this

now seize
the amulet, hurl it as far as
I can into the darkness

in which the man
vanishes. Wild as a mane
awash behind her the moon

is silver
in her hair's blonde shower
and we are rising together

each feeling
the other heave like wave and rolling
surge, and falling, falling.

The Mission Of Port Keats

At Port Keats the heat is gentle
for thirty-four, and almost dry
although we're well into the Wet
and near a creek and mangrove swamp.

Silence now. But not a moment
ago a mob of parrots squawking
overhead, we heard the brickmakers
clinking their chisels, sounds carried

then muffled by heat, as when our truck
stopped, the waiting air absorbed
its engine noise. While we are wary
of this silence, the Aborigines

chatter in their peaceful element;
in the school their children chant
in Murinbata, now the common tongue
even of the Maringar, the Murinjabin,

onetime targets of their shovel spears—
which flung with force would wham
into a fighter's back, jamming
through his ribs a skewer fist.

Inside the mission church the air
cool around a lacquered Madonna
and Child: her robe is blue, her crown
yellowy gold, the wall behind

of zinc-grey corrugated iron
which they salvaged from an army hut.
To the left, pulpit and sanctuary
backdrop painted like the altar

in ochres—their Great Emu's blood
gift to the earth, with brown and yellow
wavy lines summoning the Rainbow
Serpent, storm-bringing

herald of the mother Kunapipi,
the great sky snake who makes
the rain and rivers, who leads
the spirit children to the womb.

They say they get on with the priests,
these elders who have just made men
of twenty boys, not with the flint
or modern shard of bottle glass

but with the clean cut of a scalpel
in the hospital; two days'
corroboree outside, all the stories
acted out to the didgeridoos'

bass growling, sticks from church
rapped now with a fury reserved
for body music as the men, white-
faced like flour gods, bleed

and smear themselves, rub wisps
of down into the caking blood
to leap and dart as quick as any bird
and dance into the dreamtime.

Today they go about their work.
Those heaving barrow loads of bricks
are newcomers, men whose families
crowd in shacks at the settlement edge

until they've built them modern homes.
We're sitting in the shade: our pilot
waiting for the other passengers,
the bishop quiet, lost in thought.

The world returns to silence here:
no wind disturbs the airstrip dust,
no sound the bush that stretches out
of eyesight to the Daly River.

The pilot smacks a mossie on
his leg and curses it, then says
it's bloody quiet here; the bishop
nods, and I begin to speak.

TWO POEMS FOR MY MOTHER

Blackwood

Another still unreal day of stifling heat;
soon spent, I drooped, sweating. In Blackwood
she slept, in the mild winter she wrote about—
it had spared her plants, some were in bud.

A close night: it was ten in the morning
her time, when she reeled and dropped to the floor.
I couldn't conceive of her dying
not just as I heard, but hours before.

She'd left me on the train, feeling awkward;
vanished through the door, couldn't bear waiting.
I was to look out and wave at Blackwood.

Her last glimpse I betrayed, unknowing:
the window-lit faces rushing through the dark,
mine framed in a flash, buried in a book.

Death Telling

1. ALONE
The landlord shifted the sideboard
I didn't want. It left
a space that still holds
its shape. Like the grass

area round the corner
from here: that was a house
where a friend now dead once
lived. I still see him there.

2. BROTHER
Now I am the carrier.
My finger dials
his number to
pass on the fatal news.

My name infects him;
his voice, boyishly pleased
to hear me, like a child's
whose cry is answered.

Goannas

At dawn they'd hear it heave itself across
the ceiling, every heavy-footed thump
was greeted with a long approving hiss
as its whiplash tongue darted out to probe

where diving rafters ruled the darkness under
the roof. At first they were alarmed, no house-guest
had been mentioned; but heard then that a goanna
slept in their attic, just a jumped-up lizard

so neighbours said: no more than seven foot
from head to tail, but fatter than a barrel.
Soon it was spotted skulking in the shade
of the gum tree; inscrutable, the reptile

stared back at them, and with its tongue shot down
a gaudy dragonfly. As merciless
swiping mosquitoes as when, one by one,
it picked off victims from a scuttling mass

of cockroaches, or mopped up frantic ants,
it did not spare the praying mantises;
no insect in its path stood any chance.
I said how good it was we weren't their size.

Once I'd been swimming in the water-hole
at Berry Springs when bearing down on me
I saw the domed eyes of a crocodile.
I could not move to get out of its way

(kept up an automatic stroke), transfixed
by those determined eyes—and let it come
at me, as if the thing controlled my fate
and knew my name just as a bomb that's plumb

on target does. This monster had my number
yet at the very last veered off, no croc
after all but a rather frightened goanna.
I laughed my head off in a state of shock.

Darwin Cyclone

We weren't afraid. There wasn't time. We'd lost
the radio, and all the lights had gone.
We weren't aware of what was going on,
but watched an apparition: trees possessed

and shaking, frenzied, thrashing in the night;
watched water seeping in, creeping across
the carpet like a shadow; were shocked as
something hit the house, somewhere out of sight.

I felt the window strain and heave behind
my hand, stepped back the moment when it groaned
its shrillest note, and burst before I'd turned
the corner, running to my room to find

the wind already in the corridor.
Some flying curtains slashed me in the face.
We grabbed a mattress, shook off all the glass
and wedging it against the bathroom door

dived under it, just as a rafter broke
through, showering bricks and plasterboard on top.
Our bodies ached with crouching, water slopped
around us in the dark. We didn't speak.

The house was being torn apart with us
inside, each wall the wind was breaking down
felt like the final blow, each rending sound
the firing squad which faced us for six hours.

We didn't crack. The darkness screamed and roared.
They wouldn't shoot. I knew if we survived
I'd not want anything. Being alive
was all I thought about, until they fired.

A crack of light at dawn. The noise died down,
replaced by belting rain. Who looked out first
I don't remember, only that I raised
my head up warily. And saw. As when

someone emerges after an air raid
not knowing whether neighbours have been spared,
so I climbed up all innocent, and stared
at what I never thought I'd see outside:

a silent film of houses smashed to bits—
and streets away, in flickering rain, someone
staggering from the ruins in slow motion
(an insect crawling from its chrysalis).

The rows of trees beyond had been stripped bare.
I saw my room had gone. I had no clothes
except the things I wore, I'd lost my shoes,
and stabbed my foot before I found a pair.

I hopped about, and should have been in pain
but felt more like a dopey fool. Instead
of crying, grinned. *Hey look at me, I've cut
my bloody foot*, I shouted at the rain.

Darwin Survivor

Ten years this Christmas: never gone, not passed
over the house, the cyclone has us still
under its eye, whom it chose not to kill.
Each breath it lets us have could be the last.

With night our blindfold, a mattress to shield
each blow, we stand each shock as timber shudders
jarring through rubble. Each shriek of wind orders
our execution. I wait to be killed.

Nothing can help me now. If the next gust
wrenches a girder or some stobie pole,
and lines it up exactly with the hole
where the roof howls above, then die I must.

Anger is alien. I have no tears.
I'm grown a quiet man these past ten years.

NOTES

LOYALIST (page 14)

In his *Annales* (1625) William Camden describes how John Stubbs, 'a zealous professor of religion, the author of this relative pamphlet', was punished for his 'seditious writings' at Westminster in August 1579.

THE GREAT LOVER AT THE LAUNDERETTE (page 24)

The laundry list is not the only borrowing from Rupert Brooke's self-dramatising poem.

THE FISH (page 25)

Bidasari: a girl whose soul was kept in a golden fish. See Frazer's *Golden Bough*, LXVII. 'The External Soul in Folk-Tales'.

LISTENERS (page 27)

The epigraph quotes from a radio adaptation of Helen Thomas's *As It Was* and *World Without End*. Edward Thomas is leaving for camp.

SESTINA: ROSSETTI'S MODEL (page 30)

Rossetti's model was Lizzie Siddal, whom he met when she was eighteen, in 1850. As Millais's *Ophelia* (1852), Lizzie lay in a bath, 'her clothes spread wide and mermaid-like', and caught a chill. In her poem 'In an Artist's Studio' (1856), his sister Christina Rossetti describes the archetypal "Rossetti woman": 'One face looks out from all his canvases . . . He feeds upon her face by day and night'. A year after her death, Dante Gabriel Rossetti immortalised his dead wife as his *Beata Beatrix* (1863), 'portraiture so faithfully reminiscent,' said his brother, 'that one might almost say she sat in spirit and to the mind's eye'.

A MONTH IN THE COUNTRY (page 36)

This poem uses the voice of Mikhailo Aleksandrovich Rakitin, from
Turgenev's play *A Month in the Country*, written in Paris in 1848–50. The
other characters from the play are: Rakitin's friend Islayev, a
landowner; Natalya Petrovna, Islayev's wife; Vera Aleksandrovna, or
Verochka, Natalya Petrovna's ward; and Belyaev, tutor to Natalya
Petrovna's son. In Paris, in 1843, Turgenev fell in love with the Spanish
singer Pauline Garcia-Viardot.

ONE WAY (page 38)

The epigraphs are taken from 'Words' and 'At Galway Races', and the
quotation in line 13 from 'Under Ben Bulben'.

THE OTHER SIDE (page 40)

Orsova and *Bazias* are on the Danube, which cuts a deep gorge through
the Transylvanian Alps—the *Iron Gate*.

Kristallnacht: the night of 9–10 November 1938, when 42 of Vienna's
synagogues were destroyed by the Nazis. Hundreds of people were killed
and thousands arrested, and many houses were looted.

Post-war Vienna was divided into zones by the Allies: see the film of
Graham Greene's *The Third Man* (dir. Carol Reed, 1949), in which the
arch-deceiver Orson Welles as Harry Lime for once 'gave the impression
of stepping directly out of his own life . . . Personable bandit, in tune
with the disillusioned romanticism of the period, archangel of the sewers,
an outlaw prowling the zone dividing good from evil, a monster worthy
of love, Harry Lime/Welles was, in this case, more than a character: he
was a myth.'—André Bazin, *Orson Welles: A Critical View* (Elm Tree
Books, 1978).

Among the beasts of prey and spirits who will lay waste the land on the
day of vengeance is the *screech-owl* or night monster, identified as the
demon Lilith, who 'shall rest there, and find for herself a place of rest'
in the ruins of Edom (Isaiah 34. 14). According to Biblical
commentators, the judgement on Edom appears as an aspect of the Day
of Yahweh; Edom seems to stand (like Babylon in the New Testament)
as a type of the enemies of God's people.

In Hebrew folklore Lilith is said to have been the first "Eve", created from the earth at the same time as Adam; refusing to obey him, she fled and was turned into a demon. In post-Biblical literature she appears as a winged demon of the night, often taking on the form of a screech-owl, who kills newborn children and appears to men in their dreams; in the *Hanhagat ha-Hasidim*, an 18th century Judaeo-German book, it is said that Lilith deceives men and has children by them. And in the Talmud, Rabbi Hanina warns: 'One may not sleep in a house alone [*or*, in a lonely situated house], and whoever sleeps in a house alone is seized by Lilith' (*Shabbath*, 151b).

The widespread Jewish custom of using amulets to protect children from Lilith is explained in the Midrashic *Alphabet of Ben Sira*, where God is said to have sent the three angels *Sinoi*, *Sinsinoi* and *Semangelaf* after Lilith at Adam's request. Finding her in the Red Sea, they made her swear that whenever she saw their images or names she would lose her power over whomsoever she threatened. These "childbirth tablets" are still hung on the walls of the lying-in room in the East and in parts of Eastern Europe (Austria, Romania, Russia and Turkey).

Lilith the demon and Lilith the first wife of Adam have been conflated from separate traditions. Lilith is also identified with the Queen of Sheba (who in a Jewish and Arab myth was actually a jinn, half human and half demon). She merges with many other figures and goes under many names. In a story often included in amulets, the prophet Elijah forces her to reveal her 'eighteen or more mysterious names'. In Arabic demonology Lilith is known as *Karīna*, Tabi'a, or 'the mother of the infants'.

THE MISSION OF PORT KEATS (page 45)

Port Keats is a Catholic mission on the north coast of Australia where Aborigines from three warring tribes now live together: the Murinbata, Maringar and Murinjabin. The Great Emu, the Rainbow Serpent and Kunapipi are beings from the Dreaming, the Aboriginal time of creation. Dreamtime is eternal, an 'ever-present and immutable reality which underlines, and is expressed in, time' (A. P. Elkin, *The Australian Aborigines* [1938, 5th edition 1974]). It is re-entered in sleep and at death, through ritual and through the frenzy of corroboree dance. Procreation involves the spirit of a child being called from the dreamtime to the womb.

BLACKWOOD (page 48)

Blackwood is in South Australia, just outside Adelaide.

DARWIN CYCLONE (page 51)

The city of Darwin was destroyed by Cyclone Tracy on Christmas Day, 1974. The storm lasted for six hours, from midnight until dawn, with the strongest gusts exceeding 150 mph.

AN ENORMOUS YES
in memoriam Philip Larkin
(1922–1985)

New Poems by

Harry Chambers
Robert Hull
R. A. Maitre
Andrew Motion
Meg Peacocke
William Scammell
Vernon Scannell
David Sutton
Anthony Thwaite

PHILIP LARKIN
Two unpublished poems
Two uncollected poems
'Not The Place's Fault'
(Philip Larkin writes about his Coventry childhood)
Philip Larkin on poetry
Philip Larkin on death
Photographs
and other items from the University of Hull Larkin Exhibition

Tributes by

Peter Levi · Craig Raine · David Selzer

ISBN 0 905291 85 9   PETERLOO POETS   72 pages paperback

£4.50

2 KELLY GARDENS · CALSTOCK · CORNWALL PL18 9SA

CAUSLEY AT 70

(in honour of Charles Causley's 70th birthday)

Edited by Harry Chambers

Poems by

Alan Brownjohn ● Seamus Heaney ● John Heath-Stubbs
Ted Hughes ● Elizabeth Jennings ● Philip Larkin
Peter Levi ● Bill Manhire ● Roger McGough
Roger Pringle ● Lawrence Sail ● Anthony Thwaite
Chris Wallace-Crabbe ● David Wright ● Fay Zwicky

Prose Tributes by

Stanley Cook ● Dana Gioia ● Norman Levine
Edward Levy ● Colin MacInnes ● Barry Newport
Ronald Tamplin ● D. M. Thomas ● J. C. Trewin

CHARLES CAUSLEY

New poems
Uncollected autobiographical prose
Manuscript worksheets
Photographs & a selective bibliography

ISBN 0-905291-89-1

00495

PETERLOO POETS
ISBN 0 905291 89 1
£4.95 *120 pages paperback*

9 780905 291895

? KELLY GARDENS · CALSTOCK · CORNWALL PL18 9SA

PETERLOO

POETS

NEW TITLES 1988/89

STOCKLIST
BOOKS IN PRINT & FORTHCOMING
PETERLOO POETRY CASSETTES
ASSOCIATE MEMBERSHIP SCHEME

available (*post free*) from
2 KELLY GARDENS · CALSTOCK · CORNWALL PL18 9SA

PETERLOO POETS

"... a series kept up to scratch for a good few years by publisher Harry Chambers's energy and discrimination."
Roy Fuller/Spectator (30.1.88)

"From time to time it has seemed to me that the *Peterloo Poets* series is a haven of poetic sanity in a world of modish obfuscation."
Michael Glover/British Book News

"Harry Chambers, the publisher of *Peterloo Poets*, continues to put to shame the London publishing houses, in the flow of attractively produced volumes coming from his press. The poet who finds his major outlet in the *Peterloo* series is fortunate indeed."
D. M. Thomas/Arts South West

"I share with others an admiration for the *Peterloo Poets* imprint, particularly the way they can put the fashionable to shame and produce winners from unlikely stables."
Brian Jones/London Magazine

"*Peterloo Poets* is a small publishing house run by Harry Chambers in Cornwall. Its books are sensitively designed; each has a striking illustrated cover and the typography is excellent. The quality of production is much better than the usual standard of poetry paperbacks issued by major publishers."
G. B. H. Wightman/British Book News

"There's a solid consistency about the *Peterloo Poets* series . . . Design and printing are always excellent, and the poems themselves are never less than interesting, not least because they tend to be by people who've already done some living and have something to say."
Grevel Lindop/The Times Literary Supplement

PETERLOO POETS

2 Kelly Gardens · Calstock · Cornwall PL18 9SA